Original title:
The Symphony of Starry Laughter

Copyright © 2025 Swan Charm
All rights reserved.

Author: Lan Donne
ISBN HARDBACK: 978-9908-1-3202-0
ISBN PAPERBACK: 978-9908-1-3203-7
ISBN EBOOK: 978-9908-1-3204-4

Celestial Whimsy Carried on the Wind

Breezes dance through fields of light,
Whispers of stars in the night.
Clouds drift soft, a gentle ballet,
Carrying dreams along the way.

Moonbeams scatter like silver threads,
Illuminating paths where no one treads.
In twilight's embrace, secrets unfold,
Stories of love in the shadows told.

Each sigh from the cosmos, a shimmering tune,
Playing softly beneath the moon.
As fireflies twinkle in the dusk,
Nature hums an ancient husk.

Winds weave tales of forgotten lore,
Echoes of laughter on shores that bore.
With every breeze, a history sways,
In the celestial dance of fleeting days.

So let your heart be carried high,
On whims of stardust in the sky.
Embrace the night, let spirits entwine,
In the celestial whimsy, forever divine.

The Soundtrack of Cosmic Rapture

Stars hum softly in the night,
Melodies spin through endless flight.
Each note shines bright like a spark,
Echoes dance in the dark.

Galaxies swirl in sweet embrace,
Rhythms echo through time and space.
Nebulae paint with colors bold,
Secrets of the universe told.

Moonbeams strum celestial chords,
Harmony flows, absolving swords.
Silent whispers of the void,
In this symphony, we're overjoyed.

Comets race, leaving trails of fire,
Filling our hearts with strange desire.
The cosmos sings, a timeless art,
A rapture felt deep in the heart.

As we spin in this cosmic waltz,
Each heartbeat echoes, gently calls.
The soundtrack of the universe plays,
In its grasp, we drift in a haze.

Giggles from the Firmament

Laughter dances across the sky,
Stars giggle as they float by.
Clouds whisper secrets, soft and light,
Painting joy in the cloak of night.

Planets twinkle with playful cheer,
In the cosmos, they're always near.
Galactic giggles fill the air,
A joyful song without a care.

Meteor showers laugh in streaks,
As the universe lovingly speaks.
Twinkling lights in a playful race,
A celestial grin on each face.

Even the comets seem to smile,
As they pass through the vast, sweet mile.
In the firmament, joy takes flight,
Giggling stars shine throughout the night.

Cosmic wonder, a childlike tease,
A laughter that sweeps through the trees.
Feel the joy all around you bloom,
In the universe, we find our room.

Galactic Lullabies

In the cradle of the night sky,
Soft lullabies begin to sigh.
Moons hum gently, a soothing tune,
Stars whisper sweetly under the moon.

Nebulas swirl in pastel hues,
Dreams are born in the cosmic blues.
Galaxies spin with a velvet grace,
Carrying hopes through time and space.

Planets rest in a tranquil hush,
While stardust drifts in a gentle rush.
Each twinkle cradles a tender thought,
In the silence, dreams are sought.

The universe rocks us to sleep,
In its arms, the secrets we keep.
Celestial songs in the night unfold,
A bedtime tale forever retold.

Drifting softly on cosmic streams,
Awash in the warmth of our dreams.
Galactic lullabies calm the night,
Guiding our hearts in gentle light.

Euphoria in the Galactic Twilight

As the sun dips low, colors blend,
Twilight whispers, and worlds transcend.
Stars awaken, and shadows play,
In cosmic realms, the night holds sway.

Galactic glimmers twinkle bright,
Leading our hearts to pure delight.
Feel the pulse of the universe sway,
In this euphoria, we long to stay.

Nebulae glow in hues so rare,
A celestial dance, beyond compare.
Every heartbeat syncs with the night,
In this magic, everything feels right.

Waves of joy in the starlit sea,
Emotions flow, wild and free.
Under the cosmos, spirits soar,
In the twilight, we crave for more.

Euphoria pulses through our veins,
As constellations whisper our names.
In the galactic embrace of the night,
We find our peace in the soft twilight.

Starlight Serenade

In the night, stars softly gleam,
Whispers dance, in a silken dream.
Moonlit tales of love and grace,
Hearts entwined in a warm embrace.

Melodies across the endless skies,
Carry secrets, and gentle sighs.
Each twinkle sings a lullaby,
Awakens hopes as shadows fly.

A symphony of quiet light,
Guides the lost through the dark night.
With every spark, our spirits rise,
Connected souls with painted skies.

In the hush, we find our way,
Through the night into the day.
Starlit paths on which we roam,
In this wonder, we feel at home.

Together, in this cosmic dance,
We embrace fate, take a chance.
Starlight serenades our hearts,
As the universe plays its parts.

Echoes of Joy Among the Stars

In the void, laughter echoes wide,
Joyful whispers of cosmic pride.
Among the stars, our spirits play,
Chasing dreams that light the way.

Celestial tunes fill the night,
Guided by twinkling starlight.
Every smile, a radiant spark,
Illuminating the vast dark.

Across the heavens, our hopes soar,
Embracing all that we adore.
In this dance of vibrant cheer,
We find our joy, forever near.

As constellations weave their tale,
We ride the cosmic wind, set sail.
Echoes of laughter fill the air,
Binding hearts in love so rare.

In this realm, where dreams collide,
We chase the stars, our hearts open wide.
Echoes of joy, as we explore,
Among the stars, we yearn for more.

Radiant Giggles in a Twilight Veil

Under twilight's soft embrace,
Radiant giggles fill the space.
Stars peek through a velvet mist,
Whispers of warmth, a gentle kiss.

In this calm, we play and sing,
Joyful moments that twilight brings.
Laughter dances on the breeze,
Echoing through the rustling trees.

Every star a watchful friend,
Guiding laughter without end.
In this twilight, hearts alight,
Embracing magic of the night.

The moonbeams join our playful cheer,
Wrapping dreams, holding us near.
Radiant giggles in the dark,
Ignite our souls with a bright spark.

As night unfolds its velvet wings,
We cherish joy that twilight brings.
With every giggle, we take flight,
Beneath the stars, our spirits light.

Notes from the Cosmic Laughter

In the cosmos, where laughter sings,
Notes of joy on starlit wings.
As comets dash and planets spin,
We gather joy from deep within.

Each twinkle feels like a surprise,
A reminder of love that never dies.
In the silence, we find our muse,
Crafting tales we cannot refuse.

Galaxies hum in lullabies,
Echoing dreams beneath the skies.
Every note a spark of glee,
Weaving magic in harmony.

Through cosmic waves, we drift and sway,
Notes of laughter lighting the way.
In this dance, we lose all strife,
Celebrating the gift of life.

Together we sing, our hearts ablaze,
Caught in this cosmic, joyful haze.
Notes from laughter, a timeless tale,
Guided by stars, we set our sail.

Luminescent Emotion in the Sky

In twilight's glow, feelings soar high,
Colors blend, painting the sky.
Whispers of love caress the breeze,
Each heartbeat echoes, aiming to please.

Moonbeams dance on dreams we share,
A tapestry woven with tender care.
Stars flicker, mirth in their sight,
Illuminating the shadows of night.

Every sigh, a wish cast wide,
In the cosmos, emotions abide.
A canvas of wonder alights our hearts,
With luminescent beauty, never departs.

Floating hopes in the gentle air,
Echoes of laughter linger there.
In the vastness, we find our way,
Guided by stardust, day by day.

As dawn breaks, colors fade slow,
Yet the heart holds the glow.
In every moment, now and then,
The sky reveals its love again.

Giggles Adrift in Endless Space

In the silent void, giggles bloom,
Chasing shadows, dispelling gloom.
Stars twinkle, reflecting our cheer,
A symphony of joy, ringing clear.

Cosmic whispers float around,
Making every heartbeat a joyful sound.
Nebulae shimmer in pastel shades,
As laughter dances in glimmering parades.

Comets streak through the velvet night,
Chasing dreams that feel just right.
In each twirl, the universe spins,
Where giggles linger, magic begins.

Planets pulse to a playful tune,
Underneath the playful moon.
Galaxies swirl, an endless chase,
As we find joy in time and space.

With each twinkle, laughter grows,
In the cosmos, love overflows.
A voyage through stars, oh so vast,
In endless space, our giggles cast.

Cosmic Laughter's Embrace

In the expanse where starlight plays,
Cosmic laughter brightens our days.
Each echo like a dream untold,
Woven in tales of silver and gold.

Galaxies swirl in a joyful dance,
Carrying whispers of a sweet romance.
Planets smile in radiant glee,
As we drift in this reverie.

Meteor showers paint the night,
With bursts of joy, a dazzling sight.
Comets weave through the skies above,
Reminders of the universe's love.

As we laugh under starlit spells,
Time's gentle touch, a story that swells.
In cosmic arms, we find our place,
In a boundless world, our hearts embrace.

With every twinkle, we rise and fall,
Entwined in laughter that conquers all.
In the infinite, together we dwell,
In cosmic laughter, there's magic to tell.

Joywoven Threads of Starlight

In the fabric of night, joy takes flight,
Starlight weaves tales, dazzling and bright.
Each glow a whisper, a secret shared,
In the heart of the cosmos, love declared.

Threads of silver dance on air,
A tapestry woven with utmost care.
Cradled in constellations' embrace,
We find our rhythm, a vibrant space.

Nebulae swirl in a cosmic dream,
Shimmering softly as starlight beams.
With every pulse, hearts intertwine,
Creating a melody, pure and divine.

Joy cascades like a flowing stream,
In the vastness, we shall team.
Together we weave, forever entwined,
In threads of starlight, love aligned.

Bright the night when our spirits align,
In woven magic, we endlessly shine.
As galaxies blossom and stars ignite,
We dance through the wonders of space's delight.

The Weightlessness of Joy

Soft whispers in the air,
Floating dreams without a care.
Sunlight dances on the skin,
Where happiness begins within.

Gentle breezes lift the heart,
In this joy, we'll never part.
Moments spark like fireflies,
In the silence, laughter flies.

A child's giggle breaks the day,
Melodies in sweet array.
Clouds embrace the endless blue,
In this space, just me and you.

We linger where the colors blend,
In this bliss, our spirits mend.
Time stands still, we breathe in deep,
As the world around us sleeps.

Finding peace in simple things,
Joy, a song that softly sings.
With every heartbeat, we explore,
The weightlessness that we adore.

Festive Harmonies Among the Planets

Under starlit velvet skies,
Planets dance and harmonize.
In the night, a joyful play,
Cosmic music leads the way.

Jupiter's laugh, so vast and grand,
Echoes through the starry band.
Saturn spins with rings of light,
Creating rhythms through the night.

Mars provides a rhythmic beat,
With whispers of the red retreat.
Venus sings in sultry tunes,
Drawing wishes from the moons.

Together, they form a sound,
A melody that knows no bound.
Galaxies sway in sweet embrace,
Time and space in endless grace.

This is where our dreams align,
In the cosmos, stars combine.
With every note, we are set free,
Festive harmonies for you and me.

Glimmers of Laughter in the Ether

In the stillness, echoes play,
Glimmers shine along the way.
Every chuckle, soft and bright,
Fleeting joy, a spark of light.

Ethereal wisps of cheer,
Drift around, so crystal clear.
In every giggle, in each grin,
Laughter is where love begins.

Moments captured in delight,
Filling hearts with purest light.
Through the clouds, through the haze,
Laughter weaves a gentle phrase.

Softly swirling in the breeze,
Joy on heartstrings, it will tease.
With whispers tickling the soul,
In this laughter, we are whole.

Glimmers dance in twilight's glow,
Reminding us to always flow.
Finding magic in the air,
In each laugh, we learn to care.

Cosmic Choreography of Whimsy

Underneath the starry vault,
Whimsy spins, it finds no fault.
Galaxies twirl in playful grace,
In this dance, let's find our place.

Comets trail with laughter bright,
Painting colors through the night.
Nebulae spin with vibrant hues,
Crafting dreams that we can choose.

Asteroids waltz, a bumpy ride,
Through the cosmos, side by side.
In this ballet of the skies,
Every twirl, a sweet surprise.

The rhythm of the universe,
In every verse, we'll immerse.
With each leap, we float on air,
In this whimsy, we are rare.

Together, we'll chase the stars,
Write our names on Venus' bars.
In endless space, let's twine and bend,
Cosmic choreography, a friend.

Whimsical Whirls through the Night

In shadows where the starlight plays,
A dance of dreams begins to sway.
Whirls of whispers fill the air,
As nocturnal wonders linger there.

The moon, a guide with gentle beams,
Leads us through enchanted dreams.
In every twirl, a wish takes flight,
Chasing magic through the night.

With every step, the night unfolds,
A tapestry of tales retold.
Laughter echoes, soft and bright,
In whimsical whirls that feel just right.

Across the sky, the comets glide,
In this grand fairy tale we ride.
A world of wonder, pure delight,
Whimsical whirls through the night.

So let us dance and let hearts soar,
In a realm where dreams implore.
For in this magic, we will find,
The essence of the nighttime kind.

Laughter as Bright as Distant Suns

In fields where wildflowers bloom,
Laughter fills the golden room.
As bright as suns, their joy does spark,
Illuminating life's sweet arc.

With every giggle, spirits rise,
Like fireflies beneath the skies.
A symphony of happy sounds,
Where purest joy forever bounds.

In every heart, a light ignites,
Creating warmth on cooler nights.
Laughter dances, swift and fun,
As bright and bold as distant suns.

So gather close, feel every cheer,
For in this moment, love is near.
A bond that glows, forever spun,
In laughter's light, we all are one.

Through ups and downs, we find our way,
With laughter guiding every day.
Embrace the joy that brightly runs,
Like laughter's song, through distant suns.

Cheerful Cosmos

Stars twinkle in a cosmic dance,
Inviting dreams to take a chance.
With every glance, the universe sings,
Echoing joy that wonder brings.

Galaxies swirl in vibrant light,
Painting the canvas of the night.
In laughter's call, the heavens cheer,
Embracing all who venture here.

Planets spin in playful grace,
Creating warmth in endless space.
A cheerful cosmos, vast and free,
Where hopes and dreams can truly be.

Unruly comets dash and dive,
With spark and fire, they brightly thrive.
In this embrace of cosmic glee,
The joyful heart finds harmony.

So look above, let spirits soar,
Through cheerful worlds forevermore.
For every star's a wish that beams,
Within the cosmos, cradle dreams.

Breezes of Celestial Mirth

In gentle winds, the laughter flows,
A melody that nature knows.
Breezes whisper through the trees,
Carrying joy like a sweet breeze.

The sky, adorned with colors bright,
Gives wings to dreams that take their flight.
In every swirl, a heartbeat sings,
As mirthful echoes spread their wings.

Clouds drift by in playful tease,
Inviting peace with every breeze.
Celestial charms in twinkling views,
Unfold the joy in vibrant hues.

So close your eyes and feel the air,
A dance of joy, beyond compare.
With every breath, the laughter stirs,
In breezes filled with celestial whirs.

Let hearts unite, as spirits rise,
In the embrace of open skies.
For in this mirth, we find our worth,
In breezes of celestial mirth.

Stardust Melodies

In the velvet sky, stars gleam,
Whispering secrets of a dream.
Moonlight dances on silver streams,
The night hums softly, or so it seems.

Notes of faraway worlds take flight,
Echoing softly through the night.
Every twinkle sings a song,
A symphony where we belong.

Crickets play their gentle tune,
While shadows waltz beneath the moon.
Hearts entwined in sweet embrace,
Lost in this starlit space.

Each moment, a melody so grand,
Crafted in stillness, perfectly planned.
As we sway in the cosmic flow,
The universe whispers what we know.

Together we drift on this breeze,
With stardust whispers, our hearts tease.
In the silence, we find our bliss,
Holding onto every fleeting kiss.

Celestial Whispers of Delight

Softly the stars start to gleam,
Casting wishes on a dream.
Gentle breezes whisper low,
Guiding hearts where they must go.

In twilight's arms, we find our peace,
As shadows fade and worries cease.
The moon aligns with our sweet sighs,
In harmony, our spirits rise.

Each twinkle sparkles like a chance,
Inviting joy, inviting dance.
Celestial echoes fill the air,
As if the night itself does care.

In cosmic webs of love we glide,
With every heartbeat, side by side.
Every heartbeat sings the night,
A tapestry of pure delight.

Together, we'll wander the skies,
Find magic wrapped in midnight ties.
In every hush, in every glance,
The universe offers us a chance.

The Joyful Orchestra of the Night

Winds murmur as the stars arise,
A grand concert in the skies.
Night birds chirp in gentle tones,
Notes dance lightly on the bones.

Each star twinkles, a bright note played,
In nature's symphony, fears allayed.
Crickets strum their strings so fine,
In this divine orchestrated line.

The soft rustle of leaves in cheer,
A melody for us to hear.
The moon conducts with steady grace,
Guiding us to this sacred place.

Breezes weave a magical thread,
Where all our worries drift and shed.
Underneath this night's embrace,
Music flows with gentle pace.

So let us join this cosmic song,
A choir where we both belong.
With starlight shining bright above,
In every note, we find our love.

Radiance in the Dark

In shadows deep, a light appears,
Dispelling doubts, calming fears.
Each flicker brings a notion bright,
Illuminating the darkest night.

Stars above like lanterns glow,
Guiding paths where we may go.
A radiant dance of light and shade,
Whispers that time will not invade.

In silence, the cosmos sings,
Of uncharted journeys, endless things.
Hearts find solace in the dark,
A spark igniting with each embark.

Twinkling dreams in midnight's guise,
A place where hope forever lies.
In every gleam, a story starts,
Uniting all of our restless hearts.

Together we embrace the night,
Finding solace in the light.
For even in the darkest hour,
Love's brilliance holds the greatest power.

Nocturnal Revelations of Bliss

In the quiet night sky's embrace,
Whispers of dreams softly trace,
Stars twinkle like secrets revealed,
In darkness, our hearts are healed.

Moonlight drapes on the sleeping earth,
Each shadow dances, a moment of mirth,
Soft breezes carry laughter so sweet,
In stillness, our souls gently meet.

Gentle night cradles our sighs,
Awakening truths beneath the skies,
The world spins in a hushed delight,
Embracing the magic of silent night.

Here in this realm, worries dissolve,
In dreams, our spirits evolve,
Nocturnal bliss, a sacred art,
We find our way, follow the heart.

Galactic Giggles and Grins

Stars chuckle in the darkened void,
Galaxies twirl, dreams unalloyed,
Planets wink, with secrets they hold,
In cosmic laughter, stories unfold.

Celestial beings dance with glee,
In the vastness, we feel so free,
A nebula of joy, colors collide,
In the expanse, where hopes abide.

Meteor showers paint the night,
With trails of laughter, pure delight,
Each spark ignites a wish anew,
In the cosmos, it's me and you.

Echoes of giggles through space-time flow,
In unity, we watch and glow,
Galactic wonders unfold above,
Inviting us all to share in love.

A Chorus of Joyful Moons

Circling around in radiant cheer,
Moons of laughter fill the sphere,
Each one a note, a song to sing,
In harmony, the night awakens spring.

Silver beams dance on the sea,
Reflecting joy, wild and free,
In a symphony of shimmering light,
Together we revel in the night.

Phases change, but joy remains,
In cycles of love, no one complains,
A chorus rises with every glow,
Moonlit whispers, soft and slow.

With every heartbeat, they serenade,
In lunar embrace, fatigue will fade,
A celebration of life, every phase,
A joyful song that forever stays.

Revelry Among the Celestial Bodies

In stardust cloaked, we unite,
Revelers dance under soft moonlight,
Celestial bodies join the parade,
In cosmic bliss, our worries fade.

Comets swirl in a joyful spree,
Galaxies hum, wild and free,
Constellations twinkle with delight,
Spreading magic throughout the night.

Each twinkle a laugh, a spirit's cheer,
In the vastness, we draw near,
Infinite realms, both old and new,
A tapestry woven, it's me and you.

As nebulae shimmer and planets align,
We celebrate wonders, truly divine,
In the expanse, a joyful bond,
Revelry thrives, we're forever fond.

Gleeful Echoes of the Universe

In the silence of the night,
Whispers travel through the dark,
Stars hum melodies so bright,
Each one leaves a cheerful mark.

Galaxies spin, a twirling dream,
Colors burst in dazzling flight,
Laughter echoes in the beam,
Painting shadows with their light.

Cosmic wonders dance and sway,
Planets groove in grand parade,
Every moment, pure ballet,
In the vastness, joy is laid.

From the depths of space we hear,
Joyful sounds that intertwine,
All the universe draws near,
In a rhythm so divine.

Together we all take a bow,
In this theater of the night,
Let's embrace the here and now,
In the echoes, pure delight.

Cosmic Playfulness in the Void

In the void where shadows play,
Stars exchange a knowing wink,
Galaxies drift in bright ballet,
Painting paths where comets blink.

Nebulas burst in colored glee,
Swirling tales of light and shade,
In this vast infinity,
Joyful games of fate are laid.

Every twinkle tells a joke,
As planets spin in merry rounds,
In this cosmos, fears provoke,
Yet laughter endlessly abounds.

Beneath the blanket of deep night,
Fleeting wonders weave their charm,
Whirling gently, pure delight,
Stars embrace with open arms.

In this dance of endless grace,
We find warmth in every glance,
Cosmic play, a sweet embrace,
In this universe, we prance.

Playful Serenades of the Milky Way

In the arms of the galaxy,
Melodies of light reside,
Waves of joy so endlessly,
In the night they softly glide.

Waltzing stars in rhythmic lines,
Comets chase with playful flair,
Each note twinkles, softly shines,
Filling stillness with their air.

Shooting stars, a fleeting song,
Echo through the darkened skies,
In their music, we belong,
As we watch the heavens rise.

Milky Way, a bright embrace,
Whirls with stories yet to weave,
In this bright and sacred space,
Dreamers dance, we all believe.

To the cosmos, hearts interlace,
Finding harmony in flight,
Every pulse, a warm embrace,
In the serenade of night.

The Dance of Twinkling Stars

In the tapestry of night,
Stars begin their lively dance,
Sparkling in the soft moonlight,
Inviting dreams to take a chance.

Every flicker spins a tale,
Of wonder, love, and cosmic play,
In this waltz, we will not fail,
As the shadows softly sway.

Galactic rhythms in the air,
Swaying planets, hands entwined,
Whispers of the void declare,
In this beauty, hearts aligned.

As we watch the dance unfold,
Joy erupts in every smile,
Treasured moments softly told,
In this vast and endless mile.

Beneath the stars, we are free,
In the glow of cosmic rays,
Join the dance in harmony,
As we celebrate the ways.

Celestial Jests in Midnight's Embrace

In shadows deep, where starlights play,
The moon whispers secrets, night turns to day.
With laughter twinkling in darkened skies,
Dreams take flight, as starlit sighs.

A comet darts, a cosmic jest,
In the realms beyond, we find our rest.
Galaxies swirl in a timeless dance,
While midnight's embrace offers a chance.

Nebulas laugh in colors bright,
Echoes of joy in the velvet night.
Through the silence, their giggles ring,
In the cosmos, we find our wing.

With every breath, the universe sings,
Weaving together celestial strings.
Stars hold a mirror to our delight,
In the embrace of the endless night.

Jests of the cosmos, wild and free,
In the heart of midnight, we'll always be.
As whispers of laughter echo and swell,
Together we travel, through the starlit well.

Whispers of Joy Beneath a Cosmic Canopy

Beneath the stars, where mysteries hide,
The whispers of joy drift on the tide.
Galaxies shimmer, like laughter unspun,
Beneath the vast canopy, hearts become one.

Each twinkling light, a secret shared,
In the universe's embrace, we are bared.
With every heartbeat, the cosmos listens,
In celestial moments, pure joy glistens.

Planets murmur in delicate tones,
As stardust gathers, and laughter condones.
A symphony plays in ethereal tones,
Our spirits entwined, like ancient stones.

Under the cosmic quilt, we recline,
With dreams and wishes, our hearts align.
In the vastness, love's gentle sway,
Whispers of joy light up our way.

Together we wander, through starlit dreams,
Beneath the celestial, silent beams.
With every breath, as wonders accrue,
We dance in the night, beneath skies so blue.

Laughter Echoes in the Starlit Abyss

In the abyss where silence roams,
Laughter echoes, calling us home.
Stars twinkle brightly, watching with glee,
As night unveils its mystery.

A meteor shower, a dazzling spree,
Each flash a moment, wild and free.
Under the canvas of night's embrace,
Laughter cascades, we find our place.

Nebulae whisper in hues of gold,
Stories of joy, timeless and bold.
Together we rise through the cosmic sea,
In laughter's embrace, we simply be.

Echoes of giggles weave through the dark,
In the starlit abyss, we ignite a spark.
Every chuckle a guide, a gentle kiss,
In the silence, we find our bliss.

Through the void, our spirits unite,
In the laughter that dances, so pure and bright.
Together we drift on the waves of the night,
In the starlit abyss, everything's right.

Celestial Chimes of Mirth

In the heart of night, where echoes dwell,
Celestial chimes ring a vibrant bell.
Stars in their dance, a jubilant spree,
Whispering secrets of joyfulness free.

The universe chuckles in radiant hues,
Each note a reminder of life's joyous views.
Planets align in a cosmic embrace,
As laughter resounds, filling the space.

Under the moon, with wishes unfurled,
We bask in the magic, the wonder of worlds.
The chimes blend together, a beautiful score,
In the rhythm of cosmos, forevermore.

With giggles of starlight, we take our flight,
Through the vastness of dark, we shimmer so bright.
Mirth in abundance, a galaxy's cheer,
In the celestial realm, we hold it near.

As dawn approaches, we carry the tune,
In the heart of the night, beneath the bright moon.
With celestial chimes, our spirits ignite,
In laughter and joy, we blaze through the night.

Celestial Chimes in the Night

In shadows deep, where silence twines,
A symphony of distant lines.
Stars twinkle like a chime's pure ring,
Echoes of the night they bring.

Moonlight dances on the ground,
Gentle whispers all around.
Each note falls softly on my heart,
A cosmic song, each part a spark.

The universe hums a tune divine,
Celestial notes in perfect line.
Together under this vast expanse,
We find our rhythm, we find our dance.

In the dark, our spirits soar,
Seeking dreams and so much more.
The night unfolds, a velvet sheet,
Where time and space gently greet.

Hearts aligned with the stars above,
Wrapped in the warmth of endless love.
As celestial chimes drift through the air,
We listen close, we feel the prayer.

Laughter Beneath a Starlit Sky

In the glow of twilight's embrace,
Laughter echoes, a warm grace.
Beneath the stars, our spirits play,
In this moment, night turns to day.

Each twinkle holds a secret dear,
Whispers of joy that we all hear.
The cosmos giggles, sparkles bright,
Painting laughter against the night.

Hands held close, we share our dreams,
Beneath the moon, its silver beams.
With every chuckle, love ignites,
Filling the world with pure delights.

As constellations dance above,
We celebrate this gift of love.
With laughter bright, our hearts align,
In this starlit sky, all is divine.

Each chuckle carried by the breeze,
A melody that brings us ease.
Beneath the stars, our fears take flight,
Embraced together, all feels right.

Whispers of Cosmic Joy

Amidst the vast and endless night,
Whispers soar in softest light.
Cosmic joy, in every breath,
Echoes sweetly, life from death.

Galaxies twinkling in delight,
Share their secrets, hidden sight.
In each heartbeat, magic swells,
Starlit moments, stories tell.

In the silence, we hear the call,
Of universe, so grand, so small.
Joy is found in every space,
Every shadow, every grace.

As we wander through this sphere,
Cosmic whispers draw us near.
Hand in hand, we chase the stars,
Celebrating all that is ours.

With each sigh, the heavens sing,
In harmony, our hearts take wing.
Whispers echo through the night,
In cosmic joy, we find our light.

Melodies of the Celestial Canvas

Colors blend in twilight's hush,
Melodies swirl, a vibrant rush.
Brushstrokes of starlight paint the sky,
A canvas where dreams dare to fly.

Softly the evening's music swells,
In rhythm with the secret wells.
Each note a hue, each chord a grace,
In this vast and enchanting space.

Harmony flows, as whispers blend,
Creating a song that transcends.
Every galaxy dances in tune,
Under the watchful gaze of the moon.

Through cosmic layers, our hearts align,
In the symphony, you are mine.
Melodies of life, rich and grand,
Carrying us, like grains of sand.

In twilight's embrace, we find our place,
Colors and notes in a warm embrace.
On this celestial canvas, we dream,
Together forever, our spirits beam.

Midnight Dance of Glimmering Whimsy

In the hush of night's embrace,
Twinkling stars begin to chase.
Whispers float on moonlit streams,
Carrying our fanciful dreams.

A cascade of silver light,
Invites us to dance in flight.
Breezes twist and softly sigh,
As we twirl beneath the sky.

Each shimmer, a tale untold,
Secrets shared, and joys unfold.
With every step, the cosmos hums,
A symphony of light that comes.

Around us, the darkness sways,
As we lose ourselves in plays.
Laughter mingles with the night,
In this dreamlike, gleaming sight.

Time stands still; we dare to dream,
As stars align in radiant beam.
In this midnight dance so bright,
We find our peace, our pure delight.

Harmonic Dreams under the Celestial Sphere

Under the vast and starry dome,
Heartbeats echo, far from home.
In the quiet, music flows,
Where the essence of night glows.

Each note a brush of night's embrace,
Painting dreams in open space.
Luminous whispers call our names,
In the dance of cosmic flames.

Harmony wraps the world so tight,
As shadows merge with silver light.
In this moment, we align,
With the universe, so divine.

Stars blink softly, guiding hearts,
As celestial symphony starts.
Awake with the rhythm of trust,
In the beauty that we must.

We drift through the constellations,
Boundless dreams, endless creations.
In this sphere where spirits soar,
We find peace forevermore.

Celestial Laughter Unbound

In the night where laughter blooms,
Twinkling stars become our tunes.
Echoes of joy ring so clear,
In the realm where dreams appear.

Moonbeams dance on silver streams,
Cradling our most cherished dreams.
With each giggle, galaxies spin,
As the magic unfolds within.

Infinite laughter wraps us tight,
In the soft embrace of night.
Every chuckle lights the sky,
Painting wishes soaring high.

Together, we spin and twirl,
Through the cosmos, laughter swirls.
With every smile, a start anew,
Creating worlds where love shines through.

In this space where we are free,
Laughter echoes, a melody.
Underneath the cosmic lights,
We find joy in our flights.

Rhythm of the Infinite Night

In the stillness, shadows creep,
As the world around us sleeps.
Stars awaken with a wink,
Guiding hearts to pause and think.

The night unfolds its velvet cloak,
With every beat, a whispered joke.
Waves of silence, soft and warm,
Rock us safe from any storm.

With every breath, the night weaves tales,
Of distant lands with moonlit trails.
Echoing dreams, profound and vast,
Binding shadows of the past.

In this rhythm, souls align,
With every heartbeat, we combine.
Embracing darkness, finding light,
We dance through the infinite night.

As the cosmos hums a tune,
We twirl beneath a blazing moon.
In this union of hearts so bright,
We embrace the rhythm of night.

Starlit Revelries

Beneath the stars, we twirl and dance,
Whispers of the night's sweet trance.
With every glance, the world ignites,
In starlit revelries, hearts take flight.

The moonlight spills on dreams held tight,
Echoes of laughter, pure delight.
Each twinkle sparkles with stories shared,
In this celestial realm, we are dared.

Oh, let the night weave its silken thread,
As shadows flicker where wishes are bred.
In the embrace of the midnight glow,
Our spirits lifted, we let love flow.

Time drifts softly on wings of night,
Painting our moments in hues so bright.
In every heartbeat, in every sigh,
We find our story beneath the sky.

Starlit revelries, an endless spree,
In the dance of galaxies, wild and free.
Together we shine, a vibrant hue,
In this cosmic tale, just me and you.

Comet Trails of Joy

Across the sky, comets blaze and sway,
Leaving trails of joy, bright as day.
With each swift arc, the heart does soar,
Chasing dreams forevermore.

A burst of light, a fleeting spark,
Reminds us to shine, even in the dark.
We gather wishes in cosmic nets,
In comet trails, we chase no regrets.

Where laughter dances on every breeze,
And moments shimmer like leaves on trees.
The universe whispers tales untold,
In the warmth of joy, we break the mold.

The stars conspire in laughter's embrace,
As we dart through the universe's lace.
With every comet that brushes by,
We find our strength in the night sky.

Comet trails of joy, forever bright,
Guiding our paths with radiant light.
In cosmic wonders, together we play,
Chasing the dreams that light our way.

Universe's Joyous Performance

Among the stars, the cosmos sings,
A symphony of awe, the universe brings.
With every twinkle, a note takes flight,
In the joyous performance of the night.

Galaxies dance in a grand ballet,
Whirling with grace in a cosmic array.
Like childlike laughter, the planets cheer,
A masterpiece formed when we draw near.

In the theater of time, our hearts align,
In harmony found, we intertwine.
With stardust dreams and radiant hues,
We play our parts in this cosmic muse.

Through every challenge, we find our way,
In the universe's joy, we choose to stay.
With spirits bright and eyes aglow,
We share the wonders, let our hearts flow.

The sky's our canvas, forever in play,
In this joyous performance, come what may.
With every heartbeat, let love commence,
In the universal song, we find our sense.

Mirage of Laughter upon the Heavens

In the twilight's glow, laughter appears,
A mirage of joy that stirs our fears.
Above the clouds, where dreams take flight,
The heavens beckon us with their light.

With every giggle, the stars align,
Painting the night with a gentle sign.
In the dance of shadows, we find our way,
In mirage of laughter, come what may.

A fleeting moment, like dew on leaves,
Draws us together, as time weaves.
In every chuckle, a story unfolds,
In the laughter's embrace, our hearts are bold.

The sky erupts in a tapestry bright,
As we surrender to pure delight.
With wishes scattered like glittering sand,
In mirage of laughter, together we stand.

Above the world, where dreams collide,
In the twilight's glow, love won't hide.
A mirage of laughter, forever we'll chase,
In the embrace of the heavens, we find our place.

Enchanted Echoes in Celestial Space

Under a sky of shimmering sights,
Whispers of stars in dazzling flights.
Galaxies twirl in a cosmic dance,
Echoes of dreams in a timeless trance.

Celestial winds sing softly here,
Carrying stories from far and near.
Jewels of night graze the velvet dark,
Each twinkling light ignites a spark.

In silence, the cosmos gently breathes,
Crafting the magic that never leaves.
In every heart, the universe glows,
Enchanted echoes, a love that flows.

Jovial Symphony of the Night

Moonlight spills in a playful glee,
Creating tunes that set spirits free.
Laughter and joy fill the cool, crisp air,
Notes of the night, a melody rare.

Owls join in with their hoots so wise,
While fireflies dance like twinkling eyes.
Rhythms of nature weave a delight,
In the jovial symphony of night.

Stars sway gently in harmonious flow,
Singing lullabies that softly glow.
Together, they craft a serene embrace,
In the hearts of all, a warm, sacred space.

Trills and Thrills Beneath the Stars

In the stillness, the nightbird calls,
Echoes of trills in the shadowed halls.
Whispers of breezes, soft and light,
Enchanting rhythms that dance in the night.

Beneath the stars, excitement thrives,
Nature's song, where the magic arrives.
A chorus of crickets in gentle rows,
Creating a symphony that endlessly flows.

As dreams take flight on silvered wings,
The heart rejoices, for joy it brings.
Under the cosmos, we discover our place,
With trills and thrills, we embrace the space.

Enigmatic Chuckles of the Universe

In the vastness, secrets reside,
Enigmatic chuckles, the cosmos confides.
Stars wink knowingly, a mischievous play,
Whispering tales that drift and sway.

Galaxies spiral in curious jest,
While comets dash on a daring quest.
The universe giggles, a soft, warm sound,
In laughter and wonder, we are unbound.

Every heartbeat syncs with cosmic rhyme,
Unveiling the joy beyond space and time.
In the grand tapestry, a truth unfolds,
Life is a jest, a story retold.

Giggles Where the Comets Dance

In the night sky, comets race,
Laughter sparkles in their trace.
Children gaze with wide eyes bright,
Embracing magic of the night.

Winds whisper secrets, tales unfold,
Starlit stories, brave and bold.
With every giggle, wishes glide,
On shimmering trails, they gently ride.

Moonlight bathes the earth in gold,
Each twinkling star a story told.
Underneath these cosmic beams,
We find laughter in our dreams.

As comets dart and weave above,
We share our joy, our endless love.
In this playground of the skies,
Giggling friends where magic lies.

So let us dance beneath the glow,
Where dreams and starlight freely flow.
For every giggle shared tonight,
Is a wish on wings, pure delight.

Aurora's Giggle on Velvet Nights

In the velvet depths of night,
Auroras twirl, a wondrous sight.
Their giggles shimmer, colors blend,
Nature's laughter, a timeless friend.

Neon lights in soft embrace,
Painting the sky, the stars we chase.
Each giggle dances, whispers soar,
Creating dreams we can't ignore.

Underneath this vibrant show,
We find the warmth where giggles flow.
With every burst of greens and blues,
The heart rejoices, joy renews.

In silent woods, where shadows play,
Aurora's giggle guides our way.
A serenade both calm and bright,
Bringing dreams to life tonight.

Let the magic of the sky,
Fold us close with every sigh.
As laughter echoes in our souls,
Aurora wraps us, making us whole.

Starlit Serenade of Glee

Under starlit skies, we sway,
In the night, we laugh and play.
The moon above, our shining guide,
As giggles dance, our souls collide.

Each star a note, a song of cheer,
Whispered laughter, drawing near.
Together here, our spirits lift,
In this serenade, the greatest gift.

Voices woven, sweet and clear,
Every joy, forever dear.
With stardust dreams that never fade,
In this moment, our hearts parade.

The night embraces, soft and bright,
In starlit love, everything's right.
With every giggle, our spirits soar,
Connected deeply, forevermore.

So let us sing under the haze,
Of twinkling stars that softly blaze.
For every laugh beneath this dome,
Is a reminder that we are home.

Celestial Chortles and Cosmic Dreams

In the cosmos where laughter echoes,
Chortles ripple like gentle meadows.
Stars twinkle with a joyful gleam,
In this vast space, we dare to dream.

Galaxies swirl with playful delight,
Filling the cosmos with vibrant light.
Each chuckle a comet, bright and bold,
Stories of laughter waiting to be told.

Through nebulae of colors bright,
Cosmic dreams awaken the night.
As celestial bodies dance and play,
We find our joy, come what may.

So gather 'round, both young and old,
Let chortles weave our tales of gold.
In this universe of endless schemes,
We'll joyfully chase our wildest dreams.

In stardust trails, our laughter glows,
Azure skies where sweet love flows.
Together we'll explore and weave,
A tapestry of light, we believe.

Luminous Laughter from Beyond

In the glow of starlit skies,
Giggles dance like fireflies.
Whispers weave through cosmic light,
Echoes of the joy in flight.

Galaxies in playful sway,
Celebrate the bright array.
Laughter twinkles in the air,
A melody, both light and rare.

Waves of joy, a gentle tease,
Float on cosmic, gentle breeze.
In this realm of infinite glee,
The universe calls joyfully.

A mirthful sound from far and wide,
Where stardust and dreams collide.
Beyond the veil of night's embrace,
Luminous laughter fills the space.

So let us bask in this delight,
In laughter's glow, we find our light.
For in the joyous cosmic dance,
We're boundless souls in blissful trance.

Night Skies in Laughter

Underneath the velvet sky,
Stars alight with laughter nigh.
Moonbeams twinkle, bright and bold,
As joyous tales of night unfold.

Comets streak in playful flight,
Sparking joy with every light.
Giggles roll like waves of sound,
In the magic, we are found.

With every sparkle, dreams ignite,
Filling hearts with pure delight.
The night sings a cheerful song,
Inviting all to join along.

In this dance of cosmic play,
Let worries fade, just drift away.
For laughter weaves a gentle thread,
Through the cosmos, softly spread.

So lift your spirit to the skies,
Join the laughter, let it rise.
In night's embrace, we find our way,
Together we will laugh and sway.

Dreamy Nocturne of Cosmic Echoes

In the hush of night's soft veil,
Cosmic echoes tell their tale.
Stars entwine in dreams so bright,
Weaving laughter into night.

Here the moonlight starts to glow,
Cradling dreams in gentle flow.
Golden beams and silver rays,
Guide us through the starry maze.

Softly hums the universe,
In each giggle, in each verse.
Timeless joy meets endless space,
In this sweet celestial place.

Awake within this dreamy dance,
Let starlit wonders take a chance.
Every twinkle brings a smile,
In the cosmos, we beguile.

So let us wade through night's embrace,
Chasing laughter, finding grace.
For in the echoes, we will find,
Unity of heart and mind.

Celestial Frolic Through the Heavens

Across the skies, in swirling light,
Celestial bodies take their flight.
With laughter ringing through the air,
The universe dances without a care.

Stars perform in playful rings,
Singing songs on solar wings.
Meteor showers, a gleeful parade,
Joyous moments never fade.

Planets swirl in vibrant hues,
In wild frolic, they amuse.
Galactic laughter, vast and free,
In every corner, joy to see.

In the cosmos, dreams take flight,
With radiant smiles shining bright.
Together we will twirl and spin,
A dance of joy where all begin.

Let's soar through this starry sea,
Laughing in pure harmony.
In the heavens, love will greet,
A cosmic dance, forever sweet.

Rhythmic Radiance in the Heavens

Stars twinkle bright in the sky,
With a dance that makes hearts fly.
Whispers of light, they weave and spin,
A celestial song where dreams begin.

Moonlight kisses the quiet ground,
In this stillness, magic is found.
Each pulse of the night sings a tune,
A radiant waltz beneath the moon.

Constellations paint their tales so vast,
Stories of futures and shadows past.
In rhythm with dreams that softly swell,
The universe speaks, and all is well.

Galaxies twirl in a cosmic dance,
Inviting stardust to take a chance.
Hearts unite in this radiant glow,
As the heavens breathe and the night flows.

So let us bask in this endless light,
Finding peace in the starry night.
Each flicker a promise of things to be,
In rhythmic radiance, we are free.

Playful Harmonies of the Dark

In shadows deep, where secrets dwell,
Laughter echoes, casting a spell.
Soft breeze carries a melody sweet,
Whispers of night in a playful beat.

Dancing shadows on walls so plain,
Creating stories without refrain.
The chorus of crickets fills the air,
A symphony of moments rare.

Darkness drapes like a velvet cloak,
Where dreams awaken and spirits evoke.
With each soft rustle, a giggle takes flight,
In the playful harmonies of the night.

Stars peer down with a curious eye,
Curating tales as the world sighs.
The moon joins in with a silvery grin,
As night unfolds, let the joy begin.

Every heartbeat matches the song,
In this fleeting moment, we belong.
Playful shadows twirl, we dance in delight,
Embracing the magic of the dark night.

Galactic Giggles in Velvet Nights

In the depths of a cosmic sea,
Stars giggle softly, wild and free.
Velvet nights stretch with a gentle sigh,
As dreams ascend and spirits fly.

Planets whisper through the silence deep,
With secrets that only the stardust keep.
Galactic mirth in a cosmic breeze,
Tickling hearts with playful ease.

Nebulas burst in bursts of light,
Spreading joy throughout the night.
A canvas painted with laughter bright,
In galactic giggles, pure delight.

Time swirls on in a languid dance,
Inviting all to take a chance.
With every twinkle, a chuckle flows,
In velvet nights where wonder grows.

Stars play tag in a vast expanse,
Prompting us all to join the dance.
So let your heart laugh and take flight,
In these galactic giggles of the night.

A Night of Miraculous Melodies

The moon serenades the silent trees,
With melodies carried on the breeze.
Each note a wish, each chord a dream,
In a night of miracles, glowing like a beam.

Rustling leaves join in the refrain,
Singing stories of joy and pain.
The nightingale calls to the stars above,
In a symphony of hope and love.

The depths of night hold secrets untold,
In twinkling harmony, they unfold.
With echoes of laughter and whispers of light,
A night of melodies that feels so right.

Beneath the cosmos, we find our tune,
Dancing softly beneath the moon.
Every heartbeat sways with the sound,
In miraculous melodies, we're profound.

So let the music wrap you tight,
Through the wonders of this shared night.
As stars above our symphony weave,
In a night of miracles, we believe.

Galactic Glee in the Night's Canvas

Stars shimmer bright in velvet skies,
Whispers of light where the cosmos lies.
Galaxies swirl in a joyful embrace,
Galactic glee paints the vast, open space.

Nebulas bloom in colors so rare,
Winking comets flutter through the air.
Planets twirl in a merry round,
In this night's canvas, magic is found.

Moonlight dances with graceful delight,
Kissing the dreams that twinkle at night.
A symphony plays in the silence of stars,
Echoes of laughter from planets afar.

Each twinkle a story, each glow a cheer,
Voices of starlight, so crystal clear.
In the quiet embrace of the universe wide,
Galactic glee is our cosmic guide.

As we wander through realms of pure bliss,
Every heartbeat whispers a luminous kiss.
Together we soar on celestial streams,
In this night's wonder, we cherish our dreams.

Jovial Echoes from the Infinity

Infinity calls with a playful sound,
Echoes of joy in the universe found.
Through the cosmic silence, laughter rolls,
Jovial whispers illuminate souls.

Comets race with a gleeful grin,
Painting our hearts with the joy within.
Stars giggle softly in endless delight,
Harmonies linger, dancing through night.

In vibrant hues, the cosmos engage,
Every nebula sings, turning a page.
Worlds in motion, spinning so free,
Jovial echoes resound endlessly.

Galaxies join in a playful embrace,
Wonders abound in this infinite space.
Celestial wonders twinkle and gleam,
In cosmic delight, we awaken our dream.

With every heartbeat, we join in the cheer,
Connected through starlight, forever near.
Jovial echoes weave through the night,
In the heart of the cosmos, pure joy takes flight.

Starlit Whimsy in Cosmic Currents

A dance of starlight across the vast sea,
Whimsy flows free in this cosmic spree.
Galaxies twirl in a playful waltz,
Igniting the night with radiant faults.

Nebulas spin tales of colors so bright,
Spiraling wonders igniting the night.
In shimmering currents of cosmic delight,
Starlit whimsy takes joyous flight.

Shooting stars glitter like diamonds on high,
Tracing pathways through the infinite sky.
Laughter erupts from the planets at play,
In this grand theater where dreams sway.

The moon beams down with a nod and a grin,
Guiding the laughter where new journeys begin.
With each twinkle, the universe sings,
Starlit whimsy on luminous wings.

In the embrace of the celestial dome,
We wander together, forever at home.
Through the currents of time, we joyfully drift,
In the artistry of stars, our spirits uplift.

Laughter's Dance Among Celestial Bodies

In the night sky, laughter finds its way,
Celestial bodies in a vibrant ballet.
Stars leap and twirl with a joyous sound,
In laughter's dance, magic is found.

Planets hum softly, their rhythms align,
Echoes of joy in the cosmic design.
The universe giggles, a playful wink,
In this cosmic pond, we joyfully sink.

Asteroids join in with a playful hop,
Spinning and twirling, they never stop.
A twinkling melody fills the night air,
Laughter's dance whispers secrets to share.

The sun beams down with a warm, knowing gleam,
As stardust dances in a soft, flowing stream.
Together we sway, hand in hand through the dark,
In laughter's embrace, we're ignited with spark.

With each heartbeat, we echo the bliss,
Among celestial bodies, we dream and we wish.
In the tapestry woven through the endless expanse,
We find joy in the rhythm of laughter's dance.

Playful Stars in Joyful Reverie

In the night, stars twinkle bright,
Whispering dreams of pure delight.
Galaxies dance in sweet embrace,
Infinite wonders in time and space.

With laughter light as the gentle breeze,
They shimmer and spin, with playful ease.
Children of light in a cosmic game,
Each one a spark, never the same.

They weave their tales in twinkling glow,
Constellations forming stories we know.
A canvas vast, shimmering with glee,
Such joy and magic they bring to thee.

As shadows fade and darkness retreats,
The stars remain, with joy that repeats.
In playful reverie, they unite,
Guiding our hearts with their warm light.

Cosmic Revelry in Celestial Skies

Beneath the vast and endless night,
Cosmic wonders shine so bright.
Planets swirl in a dance so grand,
A revelry held across the land.

Galaxies twirl, in brilliant display,
A festival of lights, come what may.
Comets rush in their fleeting flight,
Celebrating existence in joyous delight.

Nebulae burst in colors bold,
Whispers of tales yet to be told.
Stars in harmony, a symphonic choir,
Filling the void with radiant fire.

In celestial skies, where dreams take flight,
The universe hums on this magical night.
A cosmic dance, forever free,
In revelry, woven intricately.

Embracing the dark with splendor bright,
Creating memories in the soft twilight.
A celebration of life, love, and cheer,
In cosmic reverie, we hold dear.

Moonlit Melodies of Delight

Underneath the silver moon's gaze,
Melodies weave through the evening haze.
Soft whispers float on gentle streams,
Carrying promises and sweet dreams.

The nightingale sings of love anew,
While shadows sway in the soft dew.
Each note a shimmer, each tone a sigh,
Moonlit music that fills the sky.

The stars align in harmonious tune,
As hearts entwine beneath the moon.
A serenade for the souls that wait,
In twilight's arms, we celebrate.

Delightful echoes dance on the breeze,
Songs of enchantment, putting hearts at ease.
With every strum, the world draws near,
In moonlit melodies, we conquer fear.

As dawn approaches, the echoes fade,
Yet the magic lingers, unafraid.
In every note, a memory stays,
Moonlit delight in countless ways.

Luminous Laughter Above the World

In the sky where the sun does rise,
Laughter glows, a bright surprise.
Above the world, joy takes flight,
Wrapped in warmth, a splendid light.

Clouds gather, soft and white,
Holding secrets of pure delight.
With every giggle that drifts away,
The sky responds in a bright display.

Children play, their voices ring,
As echoes dance, the heavens sing.
With every laugh, stars gleam with glee,
A tapestry of joy, wild and free.

The universe smiles, a glowing embrace,
Filling the void, a sacred space.
Each chuckle becomes a radiant thread,
Weaving happiness wherever it's spread.

As night descends with its gentle call,
The laughter lingers, shimmering for all.
In luminous joy, our hearts entwine,
Above the world, pure love will shine.

Laughter's Embrace in Celestial Light

Under the stars we dance and spin,
Whispers of joy wrap us in a grin.
Moonbeams shimmer in the night's delight,
Hearts are lifted in laughter's pure light.

Echoes of mirth resound from above,
Each twinkling star shines the warmth of love.
In this embrace, time gently suspends,
As night sky smiles and our laughter blends.

Clouds float softly like dreams in the air,
With every chuckle, worries disappear.
Together we weave this tapestry bright,
In laughter's embrace, all feels so right.

Catch the moments as they swiftly glide,
Ride the wave of joy, let the heart decide.
In celestial glow, our spirits take flight,
An endless journey through laughter's delight.

So here we stand, hand in hand we sway,
In the universe's grand, playful ballet.
Forever held in this luminous light,
Where laughter's embrace fills the endless night.

Celestial Carnival of Grins

A tapestry spun with threads of delight,
Under the stars, we bask in the night.
Jubilant echoes of joy fill the air,
A carnival's laughter, an effervescent flare.

Bright colors swirl in a dance of the free,
Every heart sings with jubilant glee.
Cotton candy clouds float soft overhead,
In this carnival, dreams are widespread.

Fireflies twinkle, a radiant show,
Leading us onward where laughter will grow.
In every smile, a story unfolds,
A celestial carnival that never grows old.

Together we play in this whimsical zone,
No shadows linger, feel light as a stone.
With every step, the stars start to spin,
In the joy of our hearts, let the dance begin.

So here's to the night, to the laughter we bring,
In this celestial realm, let our souls take wing.
With every grin, we dissolve all our fears,
At the carnival of grins, we embrace the years.

Celestial Chortles on Gossamer Wings

On gossamer wings, our laughter takes flight,
Carrying us high into the soft night.
Stars wink and giggle, the universe grins,
In celestial chortles, our joy never thins.

Pixies play tricks in the moonlit glow,
With every chuckle, sweet breezes blow.
Whispers of mirth tease the night's gentle ear,
As we float through the cosmos, casting off fear.

Sprinkled with stardust, our spirits ignite,
In every soft chortle, we gather our light.
The galaxies shimmer like laughter on cue,
In this magical realm, joy feels brand new.

Let the echoes of joy ripple through time,
With every sweet laugh, our hearts gently climb.
In the dance of the night, together we sing,
Out here in the cosmos, on gossamer wing.

With every shared moment, we build a safe space,
In the laughter's embrace, we find our place.
Celestial chortles, a symphony's tune,
Guided by stars, we soar past the moon.

Playful Echoes in the Night Sky

Under a canopy of shimmering stars,
We drift in laughter, forgetting our scars.
The night sky echoes our playful delight,
Filling the vastness with joy burned so bright.

Clouds dance by whimsically, soft as a sigh,
Inviting us higher as we laugh and fly.
In every moment, our spirits entwine,
In playful echoes, sweet hearts align.

The moon, a jester, glows with a grin,
Pouring out silver where the laughter begins.
A serenade woven from giggles and glee,
In the night sky's cradle, wild and free.

Each star is a wink, each shadow a tease,
We revel in folly with effortless ease.
Echoes of joy stretch far and wide,
In the night's sweet embrace, there's nothing to hide.

So let's linger here in the warmth of the night,
With playful echoes that take playful flight.
Together we bask in the starlight's soft sighs,
Lost in the wonder of joyful goodbyes.

Starlit Fables of Joy

Beneath the stars, we weave our tales,
Whispers of laughter, on night's soft sails.
Stories of dreams, in cosmic flight,
Fables of joy that dance through the night.

In twilight's glow, we find our way,
Chasing the shadows that softly play.
With every twinkle, our hearts ignite,
Crafting our hopes, in starlit light.

The moon joins in, a friend so dear,
Sharing our laughter, soothing our fear.
We sip the magic, so warm, so bright,
In this tapestry of pure delight.

Each star a spark, each burst a cheer,
Echoing laughter for all who dare near.
In the silent dance, dreams take their flight,
Starlit fables guide us tonight.

With cosmic threads, we bind our souls,
As the night sky above gently scrolls.
In every heartbeat, joy takes flight,
Starlit fables, a wondrous sight.

Jubilant Revelations in Cosmic Space

In cosmic realms where colors blend,
Mysteries whispered, secrets transcend.
Galaxies twirl in a vibrant chase,
Embracing each other with boundless grace.

Nebulae bloom, like flowers in spring,
Spreading their beauty, a joyful fling.
With stars as petals, they drift and sway,
Revelations dance in abundant play.

Each comet's tail, a vibrant trace,
Illuminates our jubilant space.
As stardust rains, our spirits rise,
In the cosmic sway, we touch the skies.

Language of light, in colors bright,
Speaks to the heart, ignites the night.
Joyful revelations in endless chase,
Whispered secrets in cosmic space.

In every twinkle, a story sings,
Of worlds unseen and the joy it brings.
Together we soar, in this infinite race,
Jubilant moments, our souls embrace.

Echoing Delight Across the Galaxies

Through the silent void, joy takes flight,
Echoing softly, a sweet delight.
Across the galaxies, a song we sing,
In every heartbeat, the universe rings.

Stars twinkle brightly, like eyes aglow,
In their embrace, our hopes freely flow.
With laughter as echoes, we dance in the night,
Spreading our warmth, in purest light.

Nebulae shimmer, a tapestry spun,
A canvas of wonder, where dreams have begun.
Each radiant pulse, a vibrant spree,
Echoes of joy that cradle the sea.

Planets align, in a cosmic embrace,
Carrying messages through endless space.
With every glimmer, our spirits ignite,
Echoing delight, a boundless flight.

From stars to worlds, our laughter flows,
In cosmic waves, where love forever grows.
Through the vastness, we pierce the night,
Echoing joy, a wondrous sight.

Celestial Constellations of Laughter

In constellations, laughter takes form,
Guiding our hearts through every storm.
Patterns of joy twinkle in space,
Celestial beings that time can't erase.

Orion's smile, a beacon bright,
Reminds us to dream and reach for the light.
Through cosmic dances, our spirits connect,
In laughter, we find what we each expect.

Cassiopeia twirls, a joyful queen,
Her laughter echoes, a radiant sheen.
In the symphony of stars, we're intertwined,
Bound by the joy that we've defined.

As comets streak, a jubilant race,
They carry our dreams across time and space.
In every burst, a memory draws near,
Celestial laughter we hold so dear.

As galaxies spin in a whirl of delight,
Our hearts embrace the infinite night.
Through cosmic realms, our love finds its way,
In celestial laughter, forever we stay.

www.ingramcontent.com/pod-product-compliance
Ingram Content Group UK Ltd.
Pitfield, Milton Keynes, MK11 3LW, UK
UKHW030857221224
452712UK00007B/1128